BIRTH,
Not Behavior

A Fresh Look at the Prodigal Son

MIKE HADDORFF | MIKE HAMEL

OTHER NONFICTION BOOKS
BY MIKE HAMEL

*The Entrepreneur's Creed: The Principles & Passions of
    20 Successful Entrepreneurs*
Executive Influence: Impacting Your Workplace for Christ
Giving Back: Using Your Influence to Create Social Change
*Stumbling Toward Heaven: Mike Hamel on Cancer,
    Crashes and Questions*
We Will Be Landing Shortly: Now What?
Social Enterprise 2.0: The OWP Difference
Spencer MacCallum: A Man Beyond His Time
Alvin Lowi Jr.: American Polymath
*Powering Social Enterprise with Profit and Purpose:
    The Tandem Hybrid*
*Meeting Homelessness with HOPE: One Community's
    Response*

BIRTH,
Not Behavior

A Fresh Look at the Prodigal Son

MIKE HADDORFF | MIKE HAMEL

Birth, Not Behavior: A Fresh Look at the Prodigal Son

Published by EMT Communications, LLC.
Colorado Springs, CO
emtcom@comcast.net

ISBN: 979-8-9870900-3-9

Cover and Interior Design: Beryl Glass

Cover Photo: Proud parents Wendell and Betty Haddorff beaming over their newborn son, Michael R. Haddorff, born March 13, 1954.

First printing—December 2023

This book is dedicated to:

My parents, Wendell and Betty Haddorff,
who gave me the opportunity to live life
and who loved me all the way,
and
Darrell Schoenig, who through decades of friendship
has shown me what it means to be a follower of Jesus.
— Mike Haddorff

Jim and Louise Wright,
my mom and dad by marriage, who modeled love and grace
throughout long lives of fruitful service.
— Mike Hamel

Contents

PREFACE

When we think about why we wrote this book, a scene from the movie *City Slickers* comes to mind. Mitch (Billy Crystal), a middle-aged guy trying to find himself, is talking with an old cowboy named Curly (Jack Palance). Curly tells Mitch about having one thing in life that's centrally important. When Mitch asks what that one thing is, Curly says it doesn't matter; it's just important to have one.

The "one thing" we want to convey in this book couldn't be more clear and straightforward; it's stated in the title: *Birth, Not Behavior*. We believe God's unconditional and relentless love for all human beings is based on our being created in his image and not on how we behave. We can't earn his love by being good or lose it by being bad.

This is the central message of Jesus' parable of the prodigal son found in Luke 15. If the title of our book is the tip of the spear, this story is the shaft that drives it home to the heart. Whether we are wandering prodigals or dutiful children, our Father loves us the same and wants to treat us the same, if only we will let him.

As simple as this message is, it is difficult for most to believe. We are unwilling to take God at his word because we see ourselves as broken. We focus on what

1

we are doing, or not doing, as the basis for relationships. We see ourselves as not measuring up or not getting all that we deserve. We don't open up to the truth that will set us free because it doesn't feel safe to be so vulnerable, even to our maker.

Jesus meant for us to see ourselves in his parables and to be changed by the truths they teach. We hope you will see yourself in our retelling of one of his most famous stories and be encouraged to embrace the "one thing" it illustrates: God's unconditional love is your birthright.

INTRODUCTION

The two authors have known each other for almost half a century, having attended a discipleship training program in California in the mid-1970s. Since then, we've followed different life paths but have remained in touch.

This book is a collaboration that has grown out of an ongoing conversation about the nature of God, humanity, and the world we find ourselves in. While many sermons have been preached and books have been written about the prodigal son, our approach is a bit different. This isn't a commentary; it's a guided meditation meant to make the three main characters in the story come alive today just as Jesus did for his audience 2,000 years ago.

Jesus originally told this tale to a mixed crowd of disciples, religious leaders, and passersby. As was true with many of his parables, there was no punch line. The listeners were left with questions to answer and argue over. It had a central message, though, which we believe is stated in the title of our book: *Birth, Not Behavior*. The prodigal son and his self-righteous older brother think and act as if their relationship with their father is based on behavior. For his part the father treats both sons based on their birth, a fact that nothing could change.

3

These three men didn't really exist; Jesus made them up. Following his example, we've made up things about them for the same reason: to flesh out spiritual truth in a way that makes it easier to understand and apply. You'll meet Lev, the son who squanders his inheritance and crawls home, hoping for a job. You'll meet Judah, his hard-working elder brother who carries the family's future on his shoulders. And you'll meet their father, Av, who loves his sons the same despite their radically different behavior.

Chapter 1 is a verse-by-verse overview of the parable of the prodigal son that Jesus taught as part of a series of three parables in Luke 15 about being lost and found.

Chapter 2 introduces the younger son, Lev, who typifies the human desire to be free from all restraints, rules, and relationships. His path from home leads downward as he encounters the Four Brutal Realities of Life. As a result, he has a change of mind and heart—repentance. As he heads homeward, the most he can hope for is to be a servant.

In chapter 3, we meet the older brother, Judah, who represents the opposite end of the human spectrum. His self-righteousness makes him judgmental of his brother and resentful of his father. He never leaves physically, but his attitude puts him outside the home once his brother returns. He has to decide if he wants to come in.

The loving father, Av, is the subject of chapter 4. He unconditionally loves his children from birth. They can't lose his love by bad behavior (Lev), or earn his love by good behavior (Judah). He is consistent and eager for both sons to come home and enjoy their sonship.

Chapter 5 takes us beyond where Jesus left off. He didn't say if the family rift was ever healed. Did the younger son really change? Did the older son ever forgive his sibling? This chapter is our guess at what could have happened next. It invites readers to apply the truths illustrated here to their life circumstances.

After our treatment of the parable, we have some back pages that include an Afterword dealing with the implications of the "allness" of God's love and Discussion Questions for groups and individuals who want to dig deeper.

Our aim is to emphasize the truth that our relationship with God is based on birth, not behavior. We can never earn or lose our Father's love, but we can live as though it is conditioned on what we do or don't do. This belief is often reinforced by religions, including Christianity, and puts a governor on our lives. A governor is a mechanical device for limiting how fast an engine can go. Metaphorically, we use it to refer to wrong ideas about ourselves and God that limit our relationship with him. More on this in chapter 2.

For example, it's common for people to say they believe in God's grace as undeserved favor. It is also common for those same people to believe their behavior makes God pleased or displeased with them. This self-applied governor limits their appreciation and experience of grace. Behavior is important, but it's not the basis of how God sees and treats us. We must recognize and resist this delusion and embrace our birthright as children of God—his eternal and unchanging love.

Now a slave has no permanent place in the family, but a son belongs to it forever. So if the Son sets you free, you will be free indeed.

John 8:35-36

It is for freedom that Christ has set us free. Stand firm, then, and do not let yourselves be burdened again by a yoke of slavery.

Galatians 5:1

1

The Three Protagonists

*J*esus continued: *"There was a man who had two sons. The younger one said to his father, 'Father, give me my share of the estate.' So, he divided his property between them.*

"Not long after that, the younger son got together all he had, set off for a distant country, and there squandered his wealth in wild living. After he had spent everything, there was a severe famine in that whole country, and he began to be in need. So he went and hired himself out to a citizen of that country, who sent him to his fields to feed pigs. He longed to fill his stomach with the pods that the pigs were eating, but no one gave him anything.

"When he came to his senses, he said, 'How many of my father's hired servants have food to spare, and here I am starving to death! I will set out and go back to my father and say to him: Father, I have sinned against heaven and against you. I

am no longer worthy to be called your son; make me like one of your hired servants.' So he got up and went to his father.

"But while he was still a long way off, his father saw him and was filled with compassion for him; he ran to his son, threw his arms around him and kissed him.

"The son said to him, 'Father, I have sinned against heaven and against you. I am no longer worthy to be called your son.'

"But the father said to his servants, 'Quick! Bring the best robe and put it on him. Put a ring on his finger and sandals on his feet. Bring the fattened calf and kill it. Let's have a feast and celebrate. For this son of mine was dead and is alive again; he was lost and is found.' So they began to celebrate.

"Meanwhile, the older son was in the field. When he came near the house, he heard music and dancing. So he called one of the servants and asked him what was going on. 'Your brother has come,' he replied, 'and your father has killed the fattened calf because he has him back safe and sound.'

"The older brother became angry and refused to go in. So his father went out and pleaded with him. But he answered his father, 'Look! All these years I've been slaving for you and never disobeyed your orders. Yet you never gave me even a young goat so I could celebrate with my friends. But when this son of yours who has squandered your property with prostitutes comes home, you kill the fattened calf for him!'

"'My son,' the father said, 'you are always with me, and everything I have is yours. But we had to celebrate and be *glad, because this brother of yours was dead and is alive again; he was lost and is found.'"*

Luke 15:11-32

Three protagonists walk into a bar. No, wait, that's a different story.

What is a protagonist anyway? And what does it have to do with the parable of the prodigal son?

A protagonist is a principal character in a literary work, the hero or heroine of a story. They drive the action, making the choices on which the story hinges. Readers are meant to see and feel the story through their eyes and emotions. The younger son gets top billing in this parable named after him, but there are three protagonists who are equally important. Their interactions are central to the narrative.

Jesus was a master storyteller, and his protagonists are well known, even to people who have never cracked the cover of a Bible. Two of his most famous parables (a Bible word for stories) are found in the Gospel of Luke: the good Samaritan and the prodigal son. The latter is one of three parables in chapter 15 that have to do with the joy of finding lost things: a lost sheep, a lost coin, and a lost son. The shepherd who rescues his sheep says, "Rejoice with me." The woman who finds her coin says, "Rejoice with me." The father who receives his son back says, "We had to celebrate and be glad."

The parable of the prodigal son has three protagonists: a younger son, an older son, and a loving father. The two brothers represent the range of human behavior, from prodigal (wastefully extravagant and foolish) to proud (self-righteous and entitled). The loving father represents the Heavenly Father whom Jesus talked so much about.

In this short story, less than 500 words, Jesus illustrated the central problem we have as humans and implied how to solve it.

The Problem: We think our relationships with God and others depend on our behavior. Some of this belief is conscious, some subconscious.

The Solution: We wake up to the fact that God loves all his children all the time. And all humans are his children.

Our behavior—good or bad—dramatically affects our ability to *enjoy our birthright*, as illustrated by the two sons in the story. Still, *it never cancels our birthright*, demonstrated by the loving father. This relational dynamic is the profound message of the parable we'll unpack in this book.

The Younger Son

"Give me what's mine, and I'm outta here!" That's what the younger son, we'll call him Lev, said to his father. Lev is short for Levi, son of Jacob and Leah, and patriarch of the priestly tribe of Levites. The Levites were scattered among the other tribes and became wanderers.

We don't know Lev's age, but he was old enough to be on his own. We'll say twenty-one. He can vote; he can drive; he can buy alcohol; he can do what he wants. And what he wanted was to be free! No rules, no restraints, no confining relationships.

"Enough of this farm life," Lev said dismissively. "There's a big, bright world out there, and I'm going to enjoy it!" If he had a theme song, it might be the famous Broadway song "I've Gotta Be Me" by Sammy Davis Jr.: "*I gotta be free, I just gotta be free. Daring to try, to do it or die, I gotta be me.*"

Once Lev got his inheritance, he wasted no time leaving the safety of home for "a distant country." He was free! But he soon learned freedom wasn't actually "free." His wild lifestyle cost him all he had. And to make matters worse, "After he had spent everything, there was a severe famine in that whole country, and he began to be in need."

The Four Brutal Realities of Life, which we'll consider in the next chapter, drove Lev from the high life to unthinkable behavior for any man, *especially* a Jewish man—living with unclean pigs and not even being able to eat with them!

Lev had lived according to the song's last verse, "Daring to try, to do it or die," and decided he didn't like the part about dying. His empty belly led to a clear mind, and Lev "came to his senses." His thoughts turned homeward. Not to the house, because he had forfeited his birthright as a son, but to the field: "Make me like one of your hired servants."

Dirty, hungry, humiliated, and humbled, Lev "got up and went to his father."

The Older Son

We think it's fitting to call the firstborn son Judah. He is named after another of the patriarch Jacob's sons. He was brother to Levi and also the founder of a tribe whose name lived on in the kingdom of Judah and the land of Judea.

Judah did everything he could to live up to his namesake. He was the typical oldest son with an inherent sense of responsibility and importance.

Born four years apart, Judah and Lev were poster boys for sibling rivalry. Their lifelong competition was fueled by birth order, temperament, opportunity, and personality. An article on the *Comprehensive MedPsych Systems* blog titled "What Your Sibling Birth Order Reveals About Your Personality Traits" noted that, "Firstborn children can be goal-oriented, outspoken, stubborn, independent, and perfectionistic . . . Youngest children can be charismatic, creative, mischievous, boisterous, and dependent on others."

True to stereotype, Judah stayed while Lev played. He worked while his brother shirked. Had he met the repentant Lev when he came crawling home, Judah might have reluctantly accepted his offer to be a servant and made him work to pay back every dime he'd squandered. Remember, what Lev selfishly spent came out of the pockets of his father *and* brother.

Mike Hamel: I have seen firsthand the sad consequences of siblings not accepting a prodigal who returns from the far country of addiction. After years of excess, this prodigal returned and sought help. She went through rehab and plugged into AA. She got a sponsor, completed the twelve steps, and made restitution where possible. She held a job and even managed a halfway house helping other addicts. She was clean and productive for more than three years and did everything asked of her.

However, her repentance and changed ways weren't enough. No matter what she did, her siblings would not accept that she had changed or that the change would last. The siblings did not want the prodigal to succeed, mainly because a child was involved. They didn't believe the prodigal deserved a second chance at parenthood. They "protected" the child and left the prodigal to fend for herself. Not surprisingly, the prodigal relapsed and disappeared, and hasn't been heard from in more than two years.

There could have been reconciliation and reunion if the siblings had accepted the prodigal back into the family and worked together toward healing. It wouldn't have been easy, but they could have helped each other toward wholeness. Instead, the siblings focused on the past, refused to be gracious in the present, and created problems for the future.

Judah wanted nothing to do with celebrating Lev's return. Instead, he "became angry and refused to go in." If anything, he was more angry with his father than his brother. Feet planted, arms folded, eyes blazing, he shouted, "What the hell are you thinking, Father? All these years I've been slaving for you and never disobeyed your orders. Yet you never gave me even a young goat so I could celebrate with my friends."

A rebellious son who left, then came back. A righteous son who stayed, but won't come in. Caught in the middle, what was a father to do?

The Loving Father
"Av" is a Jewish name for father, so that's what we'll call him. Av was industrious and successful enough to

have fields, animals, and servants. He was respected by his neighbors and was a pillar in the community. He had two sons, let's say four years apart. Mom wasn't in the picture. Perhaps she died when the boys were young, and Av never remarried.

Av built a beautiful house with his own hands; his love for his family turned it into a home over the years. Inside, his boys had everything they needed to grow and thrive. Home was a safe place for them, despite their differences. The pull of home was the pull of a safe place.

Lev looked homeward when he hit bottom. *If only I could go back home*, he thought, *even as a servant*. Perhaps he'd read the poet Robert Frost, who said, "Home is the place where, when you have to go there, they have to take you in."

Judah was drawn home when he heard "music and dancing." There had been celebrations in the house before, lots of them, but he couldn't remember any taking place in the middle of a workday. And once he learned the reason for the merrymaking, there was no way he was going to join in.

Av's boys were his life. They couldn't have been more different, but he loved them the same. He was not really surprised when Lev demanded his inheritance up front so he could sow his wild oats. Sad, but not surprised. He never gave up hope that Lev would come home one day, so he kept an eye on the horizon. Nor was he surprised that Judah devoted himself tirelessly to his duties. Valedictorian, captain of the Galilean swim team, voted most likely to succeed. And he did! He managed the estate well and increased profits every year. He was stern but fair with the servants.

Av was so proud of Judah, but that's not why he loved him. Both boys were loved before they were born. This love was their birthright. As such, it couldn't be earned or lost by what they did or didn't do.

Neither son believed it.

And that's the problem.

Mike Haddorff: I have two brothers. Chris, my youngest brother, was born when I was almost out of the house. My other brother Dave and I were fairly close growing up, being just four years apart. As younger brothers often do, Dave wanted to hang out with me. At times, this would really bug me. I thought he should be with his own friends, not with me and my friends. I didn't treat him very well on those occasions. I would often say, "Let's ditch Dave."

As we've aged, we enjoy spending time together. On more than one occasion I've apologized for how I treated him when we were kids. I feel guilty about it. One time, while Dave and I were on a fly-fishing trip in the Catskills, I started to bring up my behavior again over coffee one morning. Dave stopped me and said, "Mike, you've brought this up before. You need to know that you were a good big brother."

His kind words were a release; they meant so much to me. I got choked up and teary-eyed as I thanked him. For years I had lived with a sense of shame and guilt that I didn't need to carry. Dave's perspective was entirely different from mine. This exchange reminded me that we can sometimes feel guilt and shame for things we've done that are self-generated and limiting. How we think others think about us affects how we feel and behave toward them.

What we think God and others think about us affects how we behave toward them. When our assumptions are wrong, it's like a distortion field that warps reality, to our detriment. We'll look at this idea more in the next chapter.

2

The
Younger Son

"There was a man who had two sons. The younger one said to his father, 'Father, give me my share of the estate.' So he divided his property between them.

"Not long after that, the younger son got together all he had, set off for a distant country and there squandered his wealth in wild living. After he had spent everything, there was a severe famine in that whole country, and he began to be in need. So he went and hired himself out to a citizen of that country, who sent him to his fields to feed pigs. He longed to fill his stomach with the pods that the pigs were eating, but no one gave him anything.

"When he came to his senses, he said, 'How many of my father's hired servants have food to spare, and here I am starving to death! I will set out and go back to my father and say to him: 'Father, I have sinned against heaven and against *you. I am no longer worthy to be called your son; make me like one of your hired servants.' So he got up and went to his father.*

"But while he was still a long way off, his father saw him and was filled with compassion for him; he ran to his son, threw his arms around him and kissed him.

"The son said to him, 'Father, I have sinned against heaven and against you. I am no longer worthy to be called your son.'"

Luke 15:11-21

In our modern retelling of the parable, Lev was twenty-one, the younger son of a wealthy landowner. He hadn't lacked anything growing up, but he felt constrained and boxed in. Perhaps he acted out in his teens and was disciplined by his father. His older brother certainly neither approved of Lev's attitude and actions, nor his friends, as Lev ran with a loose crowd. Lev should have been pulling his weight on the family estate. Instead, he was more interested in doing his own thing.

Lev wanted the freedom to do what he wanted and to go where he wanted. He was old enough to strike out on his own, but he didn't have anything of his own to strike out with, so he did the unthinkable—he asked his living and healthy father to give him his part of the inheritance. Normally, this wouldn't happen until his father died. In effect, Lev said, "I can't wait for you to die; let's pretend you did and give me my share of what you've spent your whole life acquiring."

Even more unthinkable—the father granted this selfish and insensitive request.

This action would have struck Jesus' listeners as scandalous. It marked the younger son as a lawbreaker. The fifth commandment is, "Honor your father and your mother, as the LORD your God has commanded you, so that you may live long and that it may go well with you in the land the LORD your God is giving you" (Deuteronomy 5:16).

Lev dishonored his father, and it would *not* go well with him.

As soon as he could, Lev "set off for a distant country." He was doing geographically what he'd done mentally, distancing himself from home, from authority, from limits he thought others had put on him. Lev was free, but he was woefully unprepared for it. He didn't know how to budget or balance his bank account. His only investments were in food, drink, and fun. He couldn't say no to himself. It was all about the present, with no thought of the future. Live for today, and let tomorrow take care of itself.

Lev "squandered his wealth in wild living." This was how he earned the adjective *prodigal*, which means "spending money or resources freely and recklessly; wastefully extravagant." He hadn't earned the money, so he had no concept of its value. It slipped through his fingers like sand and was gone before he'd realized it.

Just when he needed a break, life pushed in as it often does. Lev came face-to-face with the consequences of his choices. His finances ran out, his friends turned away, and he wound up alone and in need. To make matters worse, "after he had spent everything, there was a severe famine in that whole country, and he began to be in need."

A young man who should have been working on his family's land and contributing to their well-being had to hire himself out to a stranger. Lev had so little to recommend himself that he was sent to feed pigs. He couldn't even earn enough to eat as well as they did. "He longed to fill his stomach with the pods that the pigs were eating, but no one gave him anything."

Lev typified the desire to be free from restraints, rules, and confining relationships. He struck out on his own from the safety of home and encountered the Four Brutal Realities of Life. They lie in wait for everyone. If you draw breath, you will encounter these truths sooner or later, regardless of race, gender, religion, or social status.

Mike Haddorff: I started Collins Control & Electric in 1980 with a pickup truck and electric drill. I was twenty-five years old. I hadn't been to college and had no business training, but I was good with my hands and knew how to work hard. I went through an apprentice-ship program and earned my journeyman and master's licenses. The business grew from small jobs for family and friends to larger homes and commercial projects.

In time, I became extremely bored with the whole thing. I felt that I was supposed to be involved with a Christian ministry and that electrical contracting was just a necessary evil. I was arrogant and didn't pay attention like I should have. When economic hard times hit in 2001, I wasn't prepared and wound up in dire financial straits. On Christmas Eve, my banker—Mr. Claus, can you believe the irony in that?—brought me in and said the bank was calling my loan. They froze all our assets and gave me thirty days to come up with the six-figure number I owed, or they would foreclose and take everything.

I had feared this moment for years. I can remember being at school plays or musicals with my kids and all of a sudden breaking out in a cold sweat. *I'm going lose it all one of these days*, I thought. But when it happened, I felt at peace about it. Something changed in me, and rather quickly. I resolved not to fight it. Still, it was a sobering, moment-by-moment time. The bank brought in someone called a "workout person" to minimize their losses. In one meeting, she wanted to know if my life insurance was paid up. "Yes," I said. "Why do you ask?"

"Well, in a situation like yours, it often comes into play."

Fortunately, it didn't. We worked well together, and she went to bat for me with the bank president. When I couldn't raise the capital to meet my initial obligation, they decided not to shut us down but to restructure the loan. Over the next six years, I made stiff monthly payments until the bank was paid off. I had to present our financial records every month and answer questions about everything. I felt like a twelve-year-old having to explain how I spent my allowance.

I wouldn't want to go through those troubled times again, but I'm glad I did. I was self-righteous and arrogant and needed to learn some lessons. This experience had a profound effect. The simplicities of everyday life became much more real and enjoyable. I started to experience what it was like to become free of me. Encountering the Four Brutal Realities up close and personal caused me to recognize and embrace gratitude and humility. When I teach them to various groups, I know what I'm talking about. And, intuitively, so do most of the men in my audience.

Brutal Reality number one: *The world does not revolve around you.* Lev learned this the hard way. He asked for his inheritance so he could be at the center of his own world and do what he wanted. He was confident, cocky, large and in charge. His outward circumstances confirmed his internal view of himself as a success. He attracted friends and collected experiences that validated his high opinion of himself. He spent money to keep up appearances until his finances ran out. He plastered over the cracks that appeared in his façade, but others saw through him and left like rats from a sinking ship.

Lev found himself less and less in control. His optimism didn't bend the world to his will, and there was nothing he could do to change his situation. His failures brought him face-to-face with Brutal Reality number two: *Life is hard.* He couldn't stay on Easy Street since he could no longer afford the rent. They say misery loves company, but Lev didn't have anyone to share his misery with because his fair-weather friends were long gone. Physical pain intruded in the form of hunger, and a "severe famine" made matters worse. He had to go to work but couldn't find a decent job. He wound up in a pigsty and envied the pigs because they had more than he did.

His journey into a distant country had been a downward spiral. From self-sufficiency to dependency.

From pleasure to pain. From full pockets to an empty stomach. It got bad enough that Lev realized he might not survive. Millions of people have starved to death throughout history, and Lev could quickly join their number, which highlights Brutal Reality number three: *You are going to die.* Most young men think they're immortal and pay little attention to death. But now Lev realized that if he didn't do something drastic, he was doomed. His bad choices could cost him his life!

At this low point, Lev was forced to confront the fourth Brutal Reality: *You are not in control.* He was in control when he asked for his inheritance. He was in control when he decided where to go and how to spend his money. But life got cruel and stripped away control. Now he was hungry and humiliated by having to do what was unthinkable for any Jew. As the article "Pigs & Judaism" by Mendy Kaminker pointed out, "There is probably no animal as disgusting to Jewish sensitivities as the pig. It's not just because it may not be eaten: there are plenty of other animals that aren't kosher either, but none of them arouse as much disgust as the pig. Colloquially, the pig is the ultimate symbol of loathing; when you say that someone 'acted like a *chazir* [pig],' it suggests that they did something unusually abominable."

Being forced out of your comfort zone and into hostile territory can happen to anyone. Financial setbacks, poor health, betrayal by a partner, the death of a loved one; the potential land mines are everywhere. In this story, Lev awakened to the Four Brutal Realities in quick succession at a fairly young age. For many people, becoming aware of them can take longer.

When Lev reached the end of his rope, he had a choice. He could assume the fetal position and adopt a "woe is me" victim mentality. He could suffer and starve in silence, all the while resenting his father and brother for not stopping him. He could spin a self-absorbed yarn in his head: *They wouldn't have let me go if they really loved me.* Looking around at his circumstances, this could be an easy conclusion to reach.

A second option was to stay the course and keep going in the same direction—away from home. His pride could take him to the next city or country where he might catch a break. He didn't have to admit defeat or tuck his tail between his legs and head home. He could shout the last couplet of William Ernest Henley's famous poem *Invictus*: "I am the master of my fate: I am the captain of my soul." Lev could endure the self-inflicted "punishments" of poverty and hunger a bit longer and pull himself up by his bootstraps. He could dig himself out of the hole he had dug himself into.

Fortunately, Lev chose a third option, and "he came to his senses." The biblical word for this is *repentance*, which means "the act of changing one's mind." Life had kicked the illusions and delusions out of Lev's head, and he could see more clearly. Instead of ignoring the pain—hard to do when you're starving—he took ownership of his choices, which we call "including the negative." He accepted the negative consequences he'd brought on himself and was able to connect the dots as to how he got where he was. Now, he could start to work on how to change his situation.

Much of the pain we experience as humans results from our unwillingness to wake up and adapt to what's occurring to us. Lev had a choice during his entire ordeal, but he had to go through what he did before he became aware of what was there all the time—the ability to choose a different path.

Before, Lev's mind was focused *away* from home, with all its restrictions and responsibilities. Now, his mind was focused *toward* home, where even the servants were better off than he was right now. He came up with a plan. "I will set out and go back to my father and say to him: Father, I have sinned against heaven and against you. I am no longer worthy to be called your son; make me like one of your hired servants."

Lev looked homeward with a glimmer of hope. He remembered his father's character. He knew enough about his father to think Av might be willing to take him back. Without that possibility, why even try? But Lev didn't assume he could return to his place as a son. The best he could ask for was to be hired as a servant. He expected to have to earn back his father's approval. Thus, he manufactured and memorized a plan.

This line of thinking reveals a "governor" Lev had created in his mind that limited his relationship with his father. We're using the word in its mechanical sense. A governor is a device for limiting how fast an engine can go. It was initially designed as a safety feature to restrict an engine's RPMs (revolutions per minute) and its overall speed. Imagine having a governor in your car that's set at 35 mph. Your engine has a lot more horsepower, but you can't utilize it. The speed limit on the interstate is 75 mph, but you can't reach it because of the governor.

Lev's governor was the idea that his father would treat him as his behavior deserved. He had cashed out his birthright as a son and spent it on selfish and reckless living. Now the most he could hope for was to be a common laborer. This governing idea was reinforced by feelings of guilt and shame: guilt at being disobedient and delinquent, and shame at what he had become. He was broke, dirty, hungry, alone, and it was all his fault!

Many of us have wrong or limiting ideas about ourselves and God that act as governors and hinder our relationship with him. We adamantly say we live by grace, but how we react daily is quite different. If you question this contradiction, consider an example: When you sin—let's assume you do—what goes through your head regarding how you think God sees you? Is he frowning? Is he disappointed?

On the other hand, when you're living as you think you should, is God smiling? Have your actions made him happy? It might be a good idea to call a time-out and ask yourself, *How is it I think about how I think about how God thinks about me?* Your governor is the unstated belief that you have to earn grace somehow. Talk about an oxymoron.

Mike Hamel: I grew up Roman Catholic. I was taught that the sacrament of baptism washed away original sin and made me a child of God. But it was up to me to stay in his good graces, and he was a strict father with lots of rules. When I knowingly broke those rules in thought, word, or deed, I had to go to confession and do penance to appease him. With my sins forgiven, I could take holy communion. Obviously, I had to be cleansed before I could receive the body of Christ into my own body.

The responsibility to stay acceptable in God's sight was on my shoulders. Enjoying my sonship was conditional on asking for and receiving forgiveness on an ongoing basis. This was definitely a behavior-based relationship. As a teenager, I often thought the best and safest way to die was to be hit by a car upon leaving church before I had a chance to sin again. The worst way to die was with an unconfessed mortal sin on my soul, for then I would be sent to hell forever.

When I became a Protestant, I was taught the same thing about original sin. All people were born in sin and unworthy of love. Forgiveness had to be earned by someone else on my behalf because God couldn't or wouldn't accept me as I was. I had to be clothed in Jesus' merit. It's called "imputed righteousness" and means God's love for me is mediated through Christ. Without him, I have no standing before God. His unconditional love has a condition—accepting Jesus. And if people don't accept him in the proper way and believe the correct things about him, God's wrath will burn against them for eternity.

Most Catholics and Protestants believe we are sinful and unlovable in and of ourselves. All humans are broken from birth and can't be loved until we are fixed, either day by day (Catholics) or once for all (Protestants). This belief is a lens distorting how we see God and ourselves. An understanding of God's unconditional love and amazing grace is needed to correct our vision.

Certainly, there's a place for repentance, confession, and restitution. Our behavior is essential and has a profound effect on our capacity to receive and interact in a healthy manner. But right behavior is the *fruit* of being loved by God, not the *root*.

We don't do anything to merit God's love, and we can't do anything to lose it. Indeed, our behavior affects our ability to enjoy our Father's love, just as Lev's behavior affected his ability to enjoy his father's love. He was starving in a hovel instead of feasting in his father's house—not because his father threw him out for his sins, but because he left home. Still, Lev's sinful behavior didn't change his birthright as a son. He would come to see this by the way his father received him when he got up the courage to go home.

That courage is seen by Lev coming to his senses. He first stopped his stinking thinking. Stopping had to come before he could start thinking clearly. Clarity could then be followed by action. This is how lasting change occurs. It also expresses the biblical idea of repentance, which means "turn." Lev had to stop before he could turn. Once he did, "he got up and went to his father." He was dirty, emaciated, ill-clothed, barefoot, and in no shape to make a good impression. But he didn't take the time to clean himself up. He knew that was impossible anyway. All he could offer was his broken self. He was humbled, shamed, and guilt-ridden, but these feelings didn't keep him from returning to his father.

As Lev began his long walk home, his gaze was probably on the ground as he trudged into familiar territory. Memories of happy times flooded his mind. If only life could be the way it was before, but Lev knew it couldn't.

That's what he thought.

His father saw things quite differently. His gaze had been on the horizon ever since his son left. That's why "while he was still a long way off, his father saw him and was filled with compassion for him; he ran to his son, threw his arms around him and kissed him."

3

The
Older Son

"Meanwhile, the older son was in the field. When he came near the house, he heard music and dancing. So he called one of the servants and asked him what was going on. 'Your brother has come,' he replied, 'and your father has killed the fattened calf because he has him back safe and sound.'

"The older brother became angry and refused to go in. So his father went out and pleaded with him. But he answered his father, 'Look! All these years I've been slaving for you and never disobeyed your orders. Yet you never gave me even a young goat so I could celebrate with my friends. But when this son of yours who has squandered your property with prostitutes comes home, you kill the fattened calf for him!'

"'My son,' the father said, 'you are always with me, and everything I have is yours. But we had to celebrate and be

*glad, because this brother of yours was dead and is alive
again; he was lost and is found.'"*

Luke 15:25-32

"Meanwhile, the older son was in the field." This open-
ing phrase accurately described the dutiful older son,
Judah. His younger brother, Lev, had wasted the family
wealth and returned penniless. His father, Av, was in the
house with Lev, celebrating in the middle of the day. Judah was working in the field just as he had been since he
was old enough to hold a hoe. He never showed up late
or left early. He didn't call in sick, even when he was.
He was proud of his family and had devoted himself to
improving and expanding their holdings.

Judah would be a type A if they had personality types
back then. He had a sense of self-importance based on
his performance. He was the one who stepped up and
carried the extra load when his brother deserted the
family. He worked so hard to overcome the impact of
losing part of the estate, which his father had foolishly
given Lev. And he'd been successful. His efforts were
paying off. Business had never been better!

Judah had yet to awaken to the Four Brutal Realities his brother had experienced. In contrast to Brutal
Reality number one—*the world does not revolve around
you*—he thought it did. He might not be fully aware

of his self-perception, but he saw himself as the one who made things happen. He held the family estate together by force of will and tireless dedication. Others saw that. They depended on him; they respected and admired him, which only confirmed Judah's high opinion of himself.

Judah was aware of Brutal Reality number two—*life is hard*—but he believed it was not too hard for him to handle. In fact, he relished the challenge! It was a point of pride that he'd faced adversity and come out on top. He was physically fit and could outwork any three men. He was emotionally stable and not subject to mood swings or impulsive behavior like his brother. Like iron forged in the fire, he'd been made stronger by the heat, not weaker.

Brutal Reality number three—*you are going to die*—was nowhere on his horizon. He was a young man in his prime, healthy as a horse, with so much more to accomplish. His father was well into his fifties, so Judah had good genes and a long life ahead of him. And Brutal Reality number four—*you are not in control*—was an outright lie when it came to him. He was in control and had the achievements to prove it. Judah did not plan to fail because he had failed to plan. He had a strategy and schedule laid out for next week, month, and year, and a five-year plan for after that. Any life coach would have been impressed.

No wonder there was a strut in Judah's step as he walked by the house on his way to check preparations for the coming harvest.

What's this? Music and dancing? At this time of day? He hadn't approved any such festivities. He stopped a servant and asked what was going on. The last thing he expected to hear was, "Your brother has come." It was like a sucker punch to the gut, followed by a roundhouse kick to the head. "Your father has killed the fattened calf because he has him back safe and sound."

Mike Hamel: I experienced the elder-brother mentality when I worked at a national organization serving churches of the Plymouth Brethren persuasion. We were on the progressive end of a conservative movement. The traditional Brethren took offense at our partnering with those who didn't do church the "biblical" way we did. Those churches had paid clergy instead of lay elders. They allowed women in certain positions of leadership instead of requiring them to be silent like the apostle Paul taught. They didn't take communion weekly. They had rock music. Their list of shortcomings was fairly long.

As a service organization, we adopted the attitude expressed in Mark 9:40, "For whoever is not against us is for us." The Brethren took the view of Matthew 12:30, "Whoever is not with me is against me."

It's okay to agree to disagree, but these elder brothers were so offended at our posture of grace and acceptance of other believers that they sued a foundation that gave us money in order to cut off our funding. They felt justified in breaking an express command in the very New Testament they claimed to defend: "If any of you has a dispute with another, do you dare to take it before the ungodly for judgment instead of before the Lord's people? . . . One brother takes another to court—and this in front of unbelievers! The very fact that you have lawsuits among you means you have been completely defeated already" (1 Corinthians 6:6-7).

The self-righteousness of elder brothers blinds them to their own unrighteousness and inconsistencies. It leads to arms crossed tightly over the chest instead of open wide to accept others.

Judah's reaction to Lev's return was the opposite of Av's. He was not happy; he was fuming! He was not celebrating; he was cursing! The situation was not only unexpected, it was totally unfair. How could his father do this? Judah was not about to go in and pretend everything was fine. It wasn't!

Just as Av went out to his younger son to welcome him home a few hours earlier, he went out to his older son with the same invitation. He pleaded with Judah to celebrate this family reunion, but Judah would have none of it. His anger at Lev boiled over onto his father. In Judah's mind, it was righteous indignation because he was being mistreated. He was indignant and shouted, "All these years . . . slaving . . . never disobeyed." And how had Av acknowledged Judah's devotion and diligent labor? He hadn't, as Judah was quick to point out: "You never gave me even a young goat." Instead, Av had rewarded the prodigal, who "squandered your property with prostitutes," with a fattened calf!

The scales weren't balanced. Anyone could see that!

JUDAH

LEV

slaved for years	didn't stick around to do his share
never disobeyed	squandered his inheritance
never even got a young goat	was celebrated with a fattened calf

Neither son got what was fair. In Judah's eyes, Lev should not be allowed back without consequences. He, Judah, should be recognized and rewarded for his labor. But Lev found forgiveness and acceptance while Judah continued to be unappreciated and ignored. This injustice was at the core of Judah's indignation.

If we put ourselves in his sandals, we might react the same way. It's natural to feel like Judah does because our default setting as humans is not grace, it's behavior, as we define it. We're the ones who classify people as in or out. The reason, ultimately, is so we can feel better about ourselves. For Lev to receive grace, instead of being shunned, soured Judah's self-righteous stomach.

After all, cause and effect make the world go round. The laws of nature—gravity, electromagnetism, etc.—are hardwired such that specific actions produce certain results. In the human realm, this is also generally how life works: the more skilled your farming, the greater your harvest. The higher your grades, the better your school and job prospects. The harder you practice, the more championships you are likely to win. When it comes to justice, you do the crime; you do the time.

Lev "did the crime" and received a pardon. Judah put in the work and received nada. His ire was understandable; how he handled it was the issue.

On the positive side, he told his father exactly how he felt. This direct and honest communication took courage and was an indicator of good mental health. A default human response would be to stuff his anger, remain silent, or stomp off and stew in his juices. But suppressing anger is like storing acid in a metal container; it eats away from the inside out.

On the negative side, Judah's outrage isolated him from the celebration going on inside. He couldn't see the blessing of his brother's return. In fact, he didn't refer to Lev as "my brother" but as "this son of yours." Av may have been reconciled to Lev, but Judah wasn't. Av gently reminded Judah of the relationship the boys shared by birth when he said, "This brother of yours was dead and is alive again."

Judah's physical distance from the celebration reflected what he'd done to himself. He had self-isolated from the joy that existed just a few steps away. He was free to go inside but stubbornly refused despite his father's pleas. It would require letting go of his anger. His refusal to do so showed the depth of human brokenness. He chose pain over freedom, hostility over joy.

In the last chapter, we pointed out that Lev had a governor on his thinking that limited how he related to his father. Lev expected Av to treat his sons as their behavior deserved, so when he returned, the best he could hope for was a lowly job. Judah had the same governor, hindering his relationship with his father. He also wanted Av to treat his sons as their behavior deserved, so when he was not rewarded for his efforts, and Lev was not punished for his offenses,

Judah was mad at Av and wouldn't enter into his father's joy.

The two sons shared the common human misconception that behavior trumps birth when it comes to our relationship with our Father. However, they are on opposite ends of the "behavior spectrum." Lev believed his bad deeds cost him the blessings of sonship. Judah believed his good deeds earned him those blessings. Both were wrong.

LEV ———————————————————— JUDAH
rebellious   BEHAVIOR   self-righteous

Their father's unconditional love was a birthright. A birthright is "any right or privilege a person is entitled to by birth." Did you catch that? Not "earned" by behavior but "entitled to" by birth.

> **Mike Haddorff:** I once had an experience that gave me deep insight into the uncompromising reality of a birthright. I was visiting a building in New York City called Edge. It has an observation deck on the 100th floor that's a triangular protrusion with a glass floor. I walked out onto it and stood suspended 1,100 feet above the street. I imagined being given a special pair of glasses that allowed me to look in both directions

from this precarious perch. As I stared up, the moon whizzed by, then Mars, Jupiter, and Saturn. The view accelerated out of the solar system, with stars warping by like in a science-fiction movie. I saw past the edge of the Milky Way and into galaxy after galaxy without end.

I took off the pretend spectacles to clear my head. When I put them on again, I looked down and saw tiny people scurrying like ants. Through the sunroof of a parked matchbox car, I glimpsed an open book on the seat. I stared through the fibrous elements of the paper down to the molecular level, where I noticed the wide open spaces between protons, neutrons, and electrons. Next came quarks and leptons floating in a bottomless vacuum.

Back on the observation deck, I pondered my little thought experiment. I became acutely aware of what is actually true. I'm in the middle of spacetime that extends infinitely in all directions. I have nothing to do with its existence, and no control over its beginning or end. But I've been born into it and get to experience and enjoy it as a birthright. This realization overwhelmed me with a deep sense of gratitude and humility.

When Lev took off, he removed himself from where he could enjoy his birthright. When he returned, it was waiting for him. His disobedience had consequences, though. The family wealth he'd wasted was gone. The scars and memories of his time in a far country would be with him for the rest of his life. Lev paid a price for his folly, but he didn't have to repay his father to get back into a relationship with him.

Av's focus wasn't on the past—what Lev did—but on the present; he came home. While Lev was away, he was still a son, but because he chose to distance himself and do his own thing, he was dead to the family. Coming back brought him in touch with the blessing of his birthright and his father's love, which had never changed.

Judah stayed put and shouldered his responsibilities without complaint, but it seems he never entered fully into his birthright. Perhaps he was so focused on proving his worthiness that he never asked his father for anything. Av showed his willingness to bless his sons by granting Lev's outrageous demand. Wouldn't he have done the same for Judah, if only he had asked?

Now Judah was the one on the outside, refusing to participate in family life. Would he listen to his father's pleading and be reconciled with his brother, or would he hang on to his self-righteousness and resentment and remain outside?

Jesus left this for his listeners to decide, but we can tell from the context in Luke 15 what he would have liked them to think and feel. He wanted them to rejoice! As Av said, "We had to celebrate and be glad." Let's have a party!

Some of Jesus' listeners would identify with being lost and then found. They were the "tax collectors and sinners" (Luke 15:1). They felt the overwhelming joy of being valuable enough to be passionately searched for and found. Others in the crowd felt differently: "The Pharisees and the teachers of the law muttered, 'This man welcomes sinners and eats with them'" (Luke 15:2).

Those who believed the father lovingly restored his unruly children would be dancing inside with the younger son. Those who expected the father to treat his children strictly as they deserved would be standing outside with the older son. The father loved both his children the same; their behavior was what made the difference between whether they could savor it or not.

Are you inside celebrating?

Are you outside judging because the situation is so unfair?

Can't make up your mind?

There was one person standing between the two sons—figuratively and literally: their father. In many ways, he's the most crucial character in this story.

4

The
Loving Father

"There was a man who had two sons. The younger one said
to his father, 'Father, give me my share of the estate.' So
he divided his property between them. . . .

"But while he was still a long way off, his father saw him
and was filled with compassion for him; he ran to his son,
threw his arms around him and kissed him.

"The son said to him, 'Father, I have sinned against heaven
and against you. I am no longer worthy to be called your son.'

"But the father said to his servants, 'Quick! Bring the best
robe and put it on him. Put a ring on his finger and sandals on
his feet. Bring the fattened calf and kill it. Let's have a feast and
celebrate. For this son of mine was dead and is alive again; he
was lost and is found.' So they began to celebrate. . . .

"The older brother became angry and refused to go in. So
his father went out and pleaded with him. But he answered

his father, 'Look! All these years I've been slaving for you and never disobeyed your orders. Yet you never gave me even a young goat so I could celebrate with my friends. But when this son of yours who has squandered your property with prostitutes comes home, you kill the fattened calf for him!'

"'My son,' the father said, 'you are always with me, and everything I have is yours. But we had to celebrate and be glad, because this brother of yours was dead and is alive again; he was lost and is found.'"

Luke 15:11-12, 20-24, 28-32

Although this story is called the parable of the prodigal son, or sometimes the parable of the elder brother, the father is actually the focal point of the tale. His behavior was the most unexpected and noteworthy. The younger son did what young men often do: go off to sow their wild oats. They do rash things that hurt themselves and others. The older son did what firstborn, responsible types do: put their noses to the grindstone and shoulders to the wheel. They take their pointy snouts and rounded shoulders as badges of honor. It's the father whose behavior was surprising.

Av should have said no to Lev's unscrupulous request for an early inheritance.

Av said yes.

Av should have waited for Lev to get cleaned up and show proper deference when he returned.

He embraced, kissed, and clothed him while he still stank.

Av should have made Lev pay back what he'd squandered.

Av gave him new clothes and a feast.

Av should have rebuked Judah for defying the summons to celebrate Lev's return.

Av reasoned with Judah instead.

Av should have compelled Judah to obey him to demonstrate his headship.

Av let Judah choose his own path, as he'd let Lev choose his.

This behavior was counter-intuitive, but so is God's love for his children. This was exactly the point Jesus was trying to make.

The parable doesn't tell us anything about Av apart from his interactions with his sons. His backstory wasn't essential for the message Jesus wanted to convey, which was Av's unconditional love for his children. This was shown by granting Lev's extravagant request to have his portion of the inheritance early, and by accepting the prodigal when he returned broken and repentant. This love was also shown in Av's non-judgmental reasoning with Judah when he refused to celebrate his brother's homecoming.

Did you notice at the beginning of the story that *both* sons received their inheritance? "The younger one said to his father, 'Father, give me my share of the estate.' So he divided his property *between them*." Lev cashed his out and took off. Judah left everything where it was; he just became the legal owner. According to the Torah, the elder son would receive a double portion of the inheritance, so Av may have given Judah two-thirds of the estate and Lev one-third when he divided his property. Some scholars believe Av maintained some ownership until his death. The details aren't important. Av's largesse enriched both sons, and both sons disrespected him by their subsequent behaviors.

In neither case did Av punish them, nor did he withhold his love until they shaped up or made amends. He didn't lay a guilt trip on them or make them feel ashamed of their shameful behavior. He didn't put them on probation or keep them at arm's length. He also didn't concern himself with what others might think about his embarrassing PDAs (Public Displays of Affection).

Av's love was like the fire that burned in the hearth in their family home. Both boys could feel the warmth and see the light when they were in the room. When Lev left for a far country, he could no longer feel or see the fire, but it never went out. When Judah refused to come into the home filled with joy, he was beyond the fire's heat and light, but it was still blazing.

What's the fuel that kept the fire burning, even when the sons couldn't, or wouldn't, enjoy it? The father's unconditional love for his children.

Av loved his sons more than life itself. That much we know from the parable. We don't know the backstory, so allow us to make one up as we have for Lev and Judah. Our hope is that fleshing out the story will help deepen its impact.

Av was a prosperous farmer and businessman. He was a respected member of his community. He had land and livestock. He was devout in his faith and devoted to his family. His wife Leah died giving birth to what would have been his first daughter, who also didn't survive. Judah and Lev were ten and six years old when they lost their mother. Her untimely death left a huge gap Av tried hard to fill.

As the boys grew into their teens, their temperaments became more obvious. Judah was the dutiful firstborn. He worked hard and excelled at whatever he was asked to do. He was fiercely committed to his family's reputation and success. He didn't need prodding from Av or seek his father's approval as motivation.

Lev went in the opposite direction as he approached manhood, shirking his duties and chafing under his responsibilities. He focused on himself, not his family.

He took their wealth for granted, even though he'd done little to maintain or grow it. His ultimate act of hubris was asking for his inheritance while his father was still alive.

We know Av granted Lev's shocking request. But why? He knew Lev's character and had a pretty good idea of what he'd do with the money. Should Av have said no and cracked down on Lev's selfish tendencies? He could have tried to force Lev to obey him, or at least not enabled his disobedience. Sometimes love says no to certain behavior, but often it allows others the freedom to receive it or reject it. Av knew Lev wasn't happy where he was; his son wanted something else. Av let Lev go, and it broke Av's heart.

Mike Haddorff: This is a story about the power of a father's love, which in my case kept me from a disastrous journey to the far country. I was nineteen or twenty and working as an apprentice electrician. I had a good job with a great employer. I was dating Sandra, who's now my wife, and I was part of a great community. But I got this harebrained idea to leave everything and take off on a nomadic trip across the U.S. I would start with what money I had, then live off the land and explore America. I was very set on this trip, and I remember getting into arguments with my parents because, of course, they thought it was a terrible idea. I spent a lot of time building my case and arguing why I needed to do this and experience this adventure of a lifetime.

I was at my folks' house one evening for dinner. My dad quietly walked into the room, and for only the second time in my life I saw tears in his eyes. That grabbed my attention. He sat down and said he wanted to talk. He reminded me how I had a great job, a bright career, a young woman who loved me, as well as a family who loved me. And yet, I was planning to give all that up for an adventure. He didn't emphasize that it was a bad idea; he just said, "I'm asking you to reconsider."

I knew how he felt because of our prior discussions. But this time, there was absolutely no point/counterpoint debate. He was sharing out of sincere love and concern for my well-being. It was only a ten-minute discussion, but one I'll never forget. It changed my mind, and I stayed home, which was the absolute smartest thing to do. I've never forgotten how love is stronger than great arguments and has the power to change behavior for the good.

Av had a pretty good idea of what would happen to Lev, so why didn't he prevent it? Wouldn't the loving thing to do have been to spare Lev the painful journey by not letting him leave in the first place? Certainly,

Av protected Lev when he was younger and immature, but boys grow into men, and wise parents know they can't control their children as they become adults.

Av's love didn't protect Lev from the consequences of his choices. Lev suffered for his sinful behavior, physically, emotionally, and spiritually. God's love for his children doesn't protect us from pain and suffering in this world. Some of it is self-inflicted. Some of it is just part of being frail and finite humans subject to illness and death. But God's love can sustain us through the pain and make us stronger for it.

Mike Hamel: God's love doesn't insulate us from the suffering that comes from being frail and finite humans. I am a cancer survivor. I had five occurrences of the Big C between the ages of fifty-five and sixty-five. I endured two stem cell transplants, sixty-plus rounds of chemo, thirty-plus rounds of radiation, fifteen-plus surgeries, and various other procedures. I blogged about my experiences, and at one point I heard from a man named Mike Rodgers, who lived in a nearby town. We had a lot in common. Both of us were pastors. Both of us were diagnosed with non-Hodgkin lymphoma the same month and endured similar chemo regimes and relapses. Subsequently, we both underwent stem cell transplants about a month apart in the summer of 2009.

In January 2011, I heard from Mike's wife, who wrote, "My Mike is now free from his lymphoma, having passed from this life on 12/25/2010."

With so much in common—positive attitudes, quality medical care, loving families, passionate prayers—why was the outcome different for us? The odds of being alive one year after a stem cell transplant are about 50/50. But who or what determines on which side of the "/" we find ourselves?

God loved both Mikes the same. That love didn't protect us from the human condition of cancer. It didn't automatically heal us when we prayed or spare us the horrors of chemo and radiation treatments. It didn't save one of us from death despite equal amounts of love and prayers from our families and friends.

We can't assume the Father's love will guarantee the outcome we want because life doesn't work that way. James and Peter were among the twelve apostles. Herod had both imprisoned. James was executed, and Peter was saved by an angel (Acts 12). It doesn't mean God loved Peter more or that more people were praying for him.

The takeaway from Acts 12, my personal experience, and instances in your own life, is not to equate God's love with specific positive outcomes, but to expect his love to see us through whatever happens.

Av allowed Lev to experience what he needed to go through. What could be seen as callousness on Av's part was really an act of love. Av risked allowing Lev to do what he wanted, even though Av knew it would harm Lev and could even kill him. Lev had to come to his senses *on his own*. His heart and mind had to turn homeward before his body could make that journey. And as soon as he did, guess who's watching and waiting?

"But while he was still a long way off, his father saw him and was filled with compassion for him." We don't know how long Lev was gone, but Av was waiting for him. Av could have felt repulsed by his son's wretched condition. Lev was dirty, gaunt, and ill-clothed; the effects of his sinful lifestyle were evident. Av could have felt self-righteous and announced, "I told you so." Instead, he felt compassion. He saw beyond the surface to the son he had always loved.

Not only was Av's heart moved with compassion, but so was the rest of him: "He ran to his son, threw his arms around him and kissed him." Av was overjoyed and couldn't contain himself. A passerby would have been shocked to see Av run. It was undignified. Gentlemen such as Av didn't run. They stood and waited for others to come to them.

Lev's pace was slow because of shame and doubt. He was skulking home with his tail between his legs, hoping for a servant's job, only to see his father running toward him, arms outstretched in welcome! Av's embrace showed more than acceptance; it demonstrated intimacy. Lev wasn't there yet, emotionally. He started with the speech he'd been rehearsing that showed his repentance: "Father, I have sinned against heaven and against you. I am no longer worthy to be called your son."

"You got that right, young man. I'm glad you learned your lesson. As soon as you make restitution, we'll talk about reconciliation." Av said none of these things. He was not only *excited* to see his son, he was *eager* to restore him to his birthright. He told the servants, "Quick! Bring the best robe and put it on him. Put a ring on his finger and sandals on his feet. Bring the fattened calf and kill it. Let's have a feast and celebrate."

The privileges of a son that Lev walked away from were restored on the spot: best robe, ring, sandals, a feast in his honor. Lev had hoped to be hired as a servant, but he's the one being served. The prodigal part of Lev's journey was over, but not the son part. He had always been Av's son, and always would be. That's what Av was demonstrating to everyone—especially Lev—with the public celebration. "Bring the fattened calf and kill it. Let's have a feast and celebrate. For this son of mine was dead and is alive again; he was lost and is found."

Av's rejoicing wasn't shared by all. It stirred the exact

opposite response in his other son. Judah was seething with anger that boiled over. "The older brother became angry and refused to go in. So his father went out and pleaded with him. But he answered his father, 'Look! All these years I've been slaving for you and never disobeyed your orders. Yet you never gave me even a young goat so I could celebrate with my friends. But when this son of yours who has squandered your property with prostitutes comes home, you kill the fattened calf for him!'"

Av could have ordered Judah to join the celebration, but he didn't. Judah was free to stay outside, just as Lev was free to leave. Instead, Av appealed to the bond the three shared as a family. Earlier, Av said, "Let's have a feast and celebrate. For *this son of mine* was dead and is alive again; he was lost and is found." Now he told Judah, "But we had to celebrate and be glad, because *this brother of yours* was dead and is alive again; he was lost and is found."

The parable ends with this appeal. We don't know what Judah decided or how Lev fit back into life on the estate. We do know that the father's love for his children was unconditional and unchanging, despite how they behaved.

And that's the point Jesus wanted to make.

5

What
Happened Next...

"'My son,' the father said, 'you are always with me, and everything I have is yours. But we had to celebrate and be glad, because this brother of yours was dead and is alive again; he was lost and is found.'"

Luke 15:31-32

After reading this parable, do you ever ask yourself, "What happened next?" Did the younger son really change? Did the older son ever forgive his brother? Did the father treat both sons the same going forward? Was the family rift ever healed? Jesus left the story open-ended, as he did with other parables. He wanted the listeners to think about their response to the situation. Would they come in and celebrate with the father at the prodigal's homecoming, or would they stay outside, aloof like the self-righteous older brother?

Which are you naturally inclined to do?

Jesus used this parable to teach a powerful lesson about God's unconditional love, which he shows all his children as their birthright, not as a result of their behavior. We want to continue the tale to emphasize the same point.

The day after the celebration, the younger son, Lev, walked through the house and saw the servants cleaning up after the feast. He had mixed feelings about being back where he grew up. There were many happy memories here before his mother died; not so many after that. He was wearing the new sandals his father had given him but his old, familiar clothes. They were nice, but they didn't fit like they did three years ago when he left at twenty-one. He'd lost a lot of weight. Not being able to afford food did that to you.

A few servants gave Lev sidelong glances. He could guess what they were thinking. *We didn't expect to see him again. Can you believe the reception he got after everything he did?*

Lev still couldn't believe it.

He went out to the porch. Two women were mending clothes and didn't hear him.

"Quite the party yesterday," one said.

"Yes," the other agreed. "But wait till the other

sandal falls. Lev won't get away with it. There will be consequences. Did you notice Av and Judah arguing and Judah stomping off? He was furious."

"Do you believe Lev will stay or take off again?"

The woman shrugged.

As Lev passed them, he said softly, "I hope he stays."

Lev played with the ring on his finger as he walked. It had been a while since he'd worn jewelry. What it symbolized about his sonship was still overwhelming. With the ring, his father showed it was as if he'd never left. What he took with him and wasted was indeed gone, but the relationship he turned his back on was unchanged when he returned.

It was a beautiful April day; the fields were ripe with barley. The wheat was coming along nicely. It had been years since Lev had been here for harvest. The crops looked good. The farm had done well in his absence. He noticed Judah talking with a group of men. *Might as well get this over with,* Lev decided. He started toward the group. When Judah spotted Lev, he turned and walked away.

Lev stopped and hung his head. He was unsure how long he stood there before he felt a hand on his shoulder. "It will take time for Judah to appreciate you being home," Av said.

Lev stared at his father. His face had more wrinkles, and his hair was thinning, but his eyes still sparkled.

"Judah has every right to be upset at me," Lev replied. "Are you?"

"I hurt for what you've been through," Av said. "But I love you the same as on the day you were born. Nothing you've done can make me love you less, and nothing you can do will make me love you more. We can use your help around here, but you have nothing to prove." He touched the ring on Lev's finger. "You are my son. That is all that matters." He opened his arms and smiled. "My heart and home are full now that you have returned." He hugged Lev. "You have gone through so much loss and suffering. You need time to heal. So does Judah. It will not be easy for him."

This conversation with Av was so different from what Lev had imagined when he was starving in a pigsty not that long ago. He remembered practicing what he would say on the long trip home: "Father, I have sinned against heaven and against you. I am no longer worthy to be called your son; make me like one of your hired servants." He only got the first part out. Av had cut him off before he could say, "Make me like one of your hired servants." He was received back as a son.

Lev still tried to wrap his head around his father's unconditional love. In the meantime, he had work to do. He joined the laborers in the field that day and every day until the barley harvest was complete. Having to hire himself out as a servant had given him a new appreciation for those who earned their bread by the sweat of their brow. He labored alongside them and got blisters like they did. He ate and slept under the stars with them. Before, he didn't even know their names; now, they were his friends.

Judah kept his distance from Lev and the fields, which was where his brother belonged. Judah had to oversee the whole operation and couldn't stoop to manual labor. There were a half dozen crops to plant and harvest from April through November, plus vineyards and orchards to manage. His workload had increased when Lev ran off, and the financial hit almost cost them the estate. The sale of herds and stored grain was barely enough to cover Lev's greedy folly. Everything could have fallen apart if Judah hadn't stepped up and saved the day. Lev couldn't expect to make things right by doing a little hard work. He had three years to make up for, plus the years he didn't pull his weight before he left.

Lev wasn't trying to earn Judah's forgiveness; he'd be happy just to be on speaking terms. Av had the family eat together most evenings, but Judah seldom spoke. He wouldn't talk to Lev, whose presence had also soured Judah's once close relationship with Av. Judah had confronted his father about coddling Lev, but Av insisted on treating Lev as though nothing had happened. "He will always be my son and your brother,"

Av often reminded Judah. "His behavior doesn't change that."

Judah sneered. "Forgive and forget."

"We won't forget," Av said. "What Lev wasted is gone. That's painful. But we can forgive. It is healthier for all of us."

"Lev's selfishness cost me a lot," Judah replied. "Cost us a lot. There's nothing healthy about that."

Judah was upset, but at least he wasn't bottling his negative emotions inside. He wasn't being passive-aggressive—that's good. But he wasn't dealing with his anger—that's not good. He still resented his father for not appreciating all he'd done. As he complained to Av when Lev returned, "All these years I've been slaving for you and *never* disobeyed your orders. Yet you *never* gave me even a young goat so I could celebrate with my friends." He believed he had a perfect right to feel wronged by his father and brother.

Still, it is healthier to forgive than to hold on to resentment. As has often been pointed out, holding on to bitterness is like drinking poison and expecting the other person to die.

At the family celebration of the Feast of Weeks, Av gave thanks for God's rich bounty. Then, he offered a special toast to Judah. "We have much to be grateful for because of your devotion and dedication, my son. This land has been in our family for generations and weathered many challenges. It has been in your hands for a while now, and I could not be more proud of how you have handled the responsibility."

Lev stood and raised his cup. "To my brother, who has carried twice the load when I did not carry my part."

Av clapped his hands, and the servants brought out a specially prepared ram and all the trimmings. Judah was dumbstruck. His father had never given him this kind of recognition before.

That evening, after everyone retired, Lev found Judah sitting by the well. "I agree with what Father said today," Lev told his brother. "You are the bedrock of this family."

"And you have been a drain on it," Judah fired back. "You broke Father's heart. Most days after you left, he would go to the top of the hill to see if you might be coming home. He did that for years! I saw the pain you caused him. And the pain you caused me, leaving me with fewer resources to keep the estate from the creditors."

"I'm sorry for what I did. It was wrong in so many ways. I hurt Father. I hurt you. I didn't realize—"

"Despite your selfishness, Father still loves you," Judah interrupted. "But don't expect any sympathy from me." With that, he got up and walked off.

Judah didn't buy Lev's "reformed sinner" act, but as the weeks passed, Judah did notice a difference. Lev was in the fields for the various harvests. Lev helped trim the grapevines and care for the livestock. He enjoyed the labor he'd once despised. He shunned the wild friends he used to hang with and attended synagogue. He was frugal with the money Av gave him and gave much of it to the poor. He hadn't forgotten what it was like to be in need.

Judah's attitude toward Lev softened as the seasons changed. Av's attitude remained constant. He loved his boys as he always had. He couldn't show it to Lev when Lev ran off, but it was there. He couldn't show it to Judah when Judah refused to accept it, but it was there.

Mike Haddorff: I came into the Vineyard Movement from the context of thinking that ministry was all about imparting information and knowledge. This is how I was taught. What captured my attention about this new experience was seeing ministry as engaging people with compassion and empathy and creating a safe place for them to get in touch with what was going on in their lives.

One night it was my turn to be prayed for, as I was struggling with feelings of shame and pent-up unmet expectations of how I thought life should be. I felt vulnerable yet safe with these people. I could be who I really was and admit what I was struggling with. I remember feeling warm hands on my shoulders while hearing the thoughtful and loving way those gathered around me quoted scriptural promises of love and acceptance. I just started weeping.

I've had similar experiences since then. Collectively, these have helped me understand that it's okay to be in pain and helpful to share that pain with others. There's no effective way to ignore pain. It will either be processed in a healthy way or rear its ugly head in unhealthy and embarrassing ways.

Over the years, I've had opportunities to pray with others about their particular needs. It's common for one's physical state to be reflective of what's occurring inside. But as they open up, their physical state softens. The lies they had believed about themselves are exposed in the light of God's truth. When they feel safe, they can remove their self-protective armor. Their bodies relax.

In our story, we see Judah open up and soften. Not in a single event, but over time as he accepts his father's unconditional love for his brother and himself. It is never scolding or shaming that brings about change. It's a safe place of love where we rest in what is actually true about us. "You have always been with me." Av demonstrated this love. Lev received it, and over time Judah did as well.

Transformation comes to us in the same way—not by striving but by receiving.

The following spring, Lev fell in love. Miriam was the youngest daughter of the neighbor to the south. They had known each other since childhood, but Miriam did not like the kind of boy Lev had been. The man Lev became was a different story. He was kind and thoughtful. He was good to the servants and the animals. He'd told Miriam about his time in the far country and what it taught him about life, and himself. It was obvious to her that the painful experience had changed him for the better.

The families approved, and the couple was married in the fall. There hadn't been a celebration like this since Lev came home. Judah attended this celebration. His wedding gift was a small house on the estate. His estate. He owned everything since Av had divided the property between his two sons; Lev had already spent his portion. Av lived in the family home as the patriarch. Lev worked for his brother. Judah had never heard him complain.

Lev was too thankful to complain. His life was so much richer than it could have been. Some nights he had nightmares of wandering alone in a strange city or scrambling with pigs for food. Then he woke to a loving family, a devoted wife, and meaningful employment on the land his ancestors had farmed for generations.

Ten months after the wedding, Lev and Miriam had their first child, a girl they named Leah after Lev's mother. Av doted on his only grandchild. Uncle Judah loved his niece to pieces. He'd been too busy to marry and had no children of his own. It turned out he liked children. Who knew? He spoiled Leah, who loved him as a second father. Her presence did a lot to heal the break between the brothers.

Leah got a brother, Aaron, two years later. Sarah joined the family in another three years, and Lev and Miriam couldn't have been happier. The estate prospered, and Judah was generous with his brother and growing family. He never gave him any land though, believing Lev lost his inheritance when it was his to control. Judah's thinking on that hadn't changed.

Years later, sadness visited the family with the death of Av at the ripe old age of seventy-six. You could say he died in the middle of Psalm 90:10: "Our days may come to seventy years, or eighty, if our strength endures."

Av left instructions to be buried beside his wife on the estate. His dying request was that Judah and Lev dig his grave and say the final blessing over his body. He had done all he could to heal the rift between his sons during his life and wanted this last act to emphasize their unity as brothers. Their lifestyle choices had been different, but they shared the same birthright, and that's what mattered.

It took Judah and Lev a few hours to dig the grave. They talked about their youth while they did. Lev admitted his mother's death had sent him on a downward spiral that ended in a pig pen in a far country. He hurt a lot of people on his descent. "It was the hardest thing I ever did to come home," Lev said when they stopped for a water break. "It was also the best thing."

"I didn't want you to ever come back," Judah said as he handed the waterskin to Lev. "But now I'm glad you did. Your time away changed you. It took me a long time to realize that. The wonderful thing about Father was he didn't need you to change before he accepted you."

"Wonderful indeed. I learned to lean into that love. I counted on it, and that made me want to please him. Not to deserve his love, but because I already had it."

Mike Hamel: One piece of advice attributed to Yogi Berra is "Always go to other people's funerals or they won't come to yours." I have followed that counsel. As a pastor, I've conducted many funerals and have buried close family members over the years: father, mother, wife, sister, brother-in-law, niece, as well as many dear friends. Funerals are reminders that death is a part of life. Few know this better than author and rabbi Steve Leder, who has presided at more than 1,000 funerals. In his book *The Beauty of What Remains*, I find words he could have spoken to Lev and Judah at Av's funeral:

That's really all they ask of us—our parents; our lovers, husbands, and wives; our children and dear friends. That we carry them gently in our lives as they carried us in theirs. Not with crushing sadness, for they do not wish such weight upon us. But with lightness and warmth. God bless them for the memories they left for us that make carrying them with joy possible. The wisdom and love they bequeathed us. The joy and comfort they brought to us as they carried us through life so that now we might carry them forever in our hearts—without bitterness, without crushing sadness. When someone has loved us well and long, we need not buckle beneath the weight of sorrow. Instead, we can carry them with us with gratitude, completeness, and joy.

The wisdom and love Av bequeathed to his sons reunited them in the end. That's the Father's desire for all his children, that we be reunited with him and all our brothers and sisters.

They completed Av's last request just before sunset and headed to the banquet being held in his honor. He was a man who enjoyed celebrations, and his family could think of no better way to say goodbye than with a feast. The brothers paused at the top of the hill and looked down at the bustling activity at the house. So many friends and neighbors had come to pay their respects.

Lev glanced the other way along the road stretching to the horizon. "This was where Father met me when I came home," he said quietly. "I didn't know what to expect when I saw him running. Was he angry and ready to lay into me? Just the opposite. He wouldn't even let me finish my confession; he just hugged me and welcomed me home."

"He said something to me when I refused to join the celebration," Judah said. "I still remember his exact words: 'My son, you are always with me, and everything I have is yours. But we had to celebrate and be glad, because this brother of yours was dead and is alive again; he was lost and is found.'"

Judah turned and grasped his brother by the shoulders. "You were lost and were found," he repeated. "I'm thankful you were."

"Me too," Lev replied. "Me too."

"The estate is mine," Judah said, "but I have no heirs. Let me say to you what Father once said to me: 'Everything I have is yours.'"

AFTERWORD

In this book, we've focused on the unconditional love of God for all his children, as illustrated in the parable of the prodigal son. This love isn't a novel idea found in a few parables; it's taught throughout the New Testament. God is inclusive in his love for humankind. We refer to this as the "allness" of God. God loves all his children all the time. We may not be able to receive that love, but it's always there, and he wants us to know it and count on it.

On one level, there are distinctions among humans, e.g., Jew and Gentile, believer and non-believer, saint and sinner, or when it comes to the parables in Luke 15, lost and found. But on a deeper level, all humans are God's children made in his image (Genesis 1:26-27; 9:6), and he loves us all the same.

The "allness" of God's love can be seen in the "allness" of his plan of redemption. Here are twenty verses from the New Testament that imply or clearly state that God's love will triumph and the redemptive work accomplished by Jesus will win out over sin and rebellion.

In the same way your Father in heaven is not willing that any of these little ones should perish. (Matthew 18:14)

For God did not send his Son into the world to condemn the world, but to save the world through him. (John 3:17)

And I, when I am lifted up from the earth, will draw all people to myself. (John 12:32)

If anyone hears my words but does not keep them, I do not judge that person. For I did not come to judge the world, but to save the world. (John 12:47)

For you granted him authority over all people that he might give eternal life to all those you have given him. (John 17:2)

Consequently, just as one trespass resulted in condemnation for all people, so also one righteous act resulted in justification and life for all people. For just as through the disobedience of the one man the many were made sinners, so also through the obedience of the one man the many will be made righteous. (Romans 5:18-19)

For God has bound everyone over to disobedience so that he may have mercy on them all. (Romans 11:32)

For as in Adam all die, so in Christ all will be made alive. (1 Corinthians 15:22)

For Christ's love compels us, because we are convinced that one died for all, and therefore all died. (2 Corinthians 5:14)

That God was reconciling the world to himself in Christ, not counting people's sins against them. And he has committed to us the message of reconciliation. (2 Corinthians 5:19)

He made known to us the mystery of his will according to his good pleasure, which he purposed in Christ, to be put into effect when the times reach their fulfillment—to bring unity to all things in heaven and on earth under Christ. (Ephesians 1:9-10)

Therefore God exalted him to the highest place and gave him the name that is above every name, that at the name of Jesus every knee should bow, in heaven and on earth and under the earth, and every tongue acknowledge that Jesus Christ is Lord, to the glory of God the Father. (Philippians 2:9-11)

For God was pleased to have all his fullness dwell in him, and through him to reconcile to himself all things, whether things on earth or things in heaven, by making peace through his blood, shed on the cross. (Colossians 1:19-20)

To them God has chosen to make known among the Gentiles the glorious riches of this mystery, which is Christ in you, the hope of glory. He is the one we proclaim, admonishing and teaching everyone with all wisdom, so that we may present everyone fully mature in Christ. (Colossians 1:27-28)

This is good, and pleases God our Savior, who wants all people to be saved and to come to a knowledge of the truth. For there is one God and one mediator between God and mankind, the man Christ Jesus, who gave himself as a ransom for all people. (1 Timothy 2:3-6)

That is why we labor and strive, because we have put our hope in the living God, who is the Savior of all people, and especially of those who believe. (1 Timothy 4:10)

But we do see Jesus, who was made lower than the angels for a little while, now crowned with glory and honor because he suffered death, so that by the grace of God he might taste death for everyone. (Hebrews 2:9)

The Lord is not slow in keeping his promise, as some understand slowness. Instead he is patient with you, not wanting anyone to perish, but everyone to come to repentance. (2 Peter 3:9)

He is the atoning sacrifice for our sins, and not only for ours but also for the sins of the whole world. (1 John 2:2)

And we have seen and testify that the Father has sent his Son to be the Savior of the world. (1 John 4:14)

These verses aren't all the Bible says regarding redemption and reconciliation, and there are differences of opinion as to the ultimate scope of God's love. Some believe God's hands are tied by his nature; his justice must be satisfied. Others believe his love can be defeated in the end by defiant human will or satanic interference. Still others believe God's will will be done, on earth as it is in heaven.

As you meditate on the parable of the prodigal son in light of these verses, what do you think?

ACKNOWLEDGMENTS

I, Mike Haddorff, along with lots of helpful friends, started Christ in the Rockies (CITR) in 2005 to engage and encourage men in their masculine journey. This book has grown out of that ministry and captures one of the central truths we teach: God's love is our unconditional birthright. When I began listing the people who have contributed to me and this effort over the years, I stopped at around 150 names. I could've kept going until my hand fell off. There are literally hundreds of board and staff members, supporters, volunteers, campers, and friends of CITR. The circle is even wider of those who have impacted my personal life. Now, the danger of trying to list everyone is that this section would be too long, and I'm bound to forget some key people. So, I'd like to thank these individuals in three broad groups.

The founding board members who believed in me and the idea of Christ in the Rockies. And for those who have served on the board over the years, many for more than one term. I'm forever grateful for your support.

Early financial supporters who shared the cost of creating an entity, designing a website, buying insurance, and other miscellaneous expenses of incorporating and starting a nonprofit ministry. And to our financial donors who have invested in the vision year after year.

The scores and scores of volunteers who have helped with the nuts and bolts and heavy lifting of setting up and taking down several camps each year—over and over and over again.

I do want to mention by name the individuals who made this book possible: Tim Strickland, Linda Vomaske, Rob Strouse, Tim FitzGerald, Jim Zalenski, and Steve Brown.

RECOMMENDED READING

Timothy Keller, *The Prodigal God: Recovering the Heart of the Christian Faith*, (London: Penguin Books; reprint edition, 2011).

Henri J. M. Nouwen, *The Return of the Prodigal Son: A Story of Homecoming*, (New York: Crown Publishing Group, 1994).

Philip Yancey, *What's So Amazing About Grace?*, (Grand Rapids, MI: Zondervan, 2002).

Peter Enns, *How the Bible Actually Works: In Which I Explain How An Ancient, Ambiguous, and Diverse Book Leads Us to Wisdom Rather Than Answers—and Why That's Great News* (San Francisco: HarperOne, 2019).

Richard Rohr, *Breathing Under Water: Spirituality and the Twelve Steps*, (Cincinnati: Franciscan Media, 2021).

DISCUSSION QUESTIONS

Chapter 1 | Three Protagonists

Group Discussion

1. Why did Av grant Lev's selfish request even though he knew it would lead to painful failure and the brink of death?

2. To what degree do you think the human default setting is that our relationship with God is based on our behavior?

3. All humans are made in the image of God, but are all humans his children and objects of his unconditional love? If so, what are some implications?

Going Inward

How do you think your behavior affects how God thinks about you? Set a timer for ten minutes and start writing about this question until the time is up. For your eyes only, don't worry about what comes out; just get your initial thoughts down.

Chapter 2 | The Younger Son

Group Discussion

Lev's experiences illustrate the Four Brutal Realities of Life. We believe they are universal and unavoidable, although people experience them to different degrees and at different stages in life. Answer these questions based on where you're currently at in your personal journey:

1. Brutal Reality number one: *The world does not revolve around you.* Have you encountered this reality? If so, what were the circumstances, and what lessons did you draw from your experience?

2. Brutal Reality number two: *Life is hard.* Have you encountered this reality? If so, what were the circumstances, and what lessons did you draw from your experience?

3. Brutal Reality number three: *You are going to die.* Have you encountered this reality? If so, what were the circumstances, and what lessons did you draw from your experience?

4. Brutal Reality number four: *You are not in control.* Have you encountered this reality? If so, what were the circumstances, and what lessons did you draw from your experience?

Going Inward

Identify one of the Four Brutal Realities that seems the most prominent where you're at in your journey right now. What difference would it make in your thinking and behavior if you accepted this reality as something you can't change? Set a timer for ten minutes and start writing about this question until the time is up. For your eyes only, don't worry about what comes out; just get your initial thoughts down.

Chapter 3 | The Older Son

Group Discussion

1. Both Lev and Judah had a governor on their thinking in the common misconception that behavior overshadows birth when it came to their relationship with their father. However, they were on opposite ends of the behavior spectrum. What did Lev believe? What did Judah believe?

Lev _____ Judah

Behavior Spectrum

2. We don't talk about it much today, but what is a birthright? How can a birthright be affected by behavior?

3. If you were in Judah's position, would you go inside and join the celebration, or would you ignore Av's pleas and stay outside? How would you explain your actions to a bystander?

Going Inward

In what ways can you see your thinking and feelings as you reflect on this front porch interaction between Judah and Av? Set a timer for ten minutes and start writing about this question until the time is up. For your eyes only, don't worry about what comes out; just get your initial thoughts down.

Chapter 4 | The Loving Father

Group Discussion

1. What did you find surprising and unexpected about Av's behavior toward Lev? Toward Judah? See if you can come up with at least six of Av's actions that would have shocked Jesus' original listeners.

2. What role did Lev's repentance play in Av's reception of his prodigal son? What role does repentance play in our relationship with the Heavenly Father?

3. Why didn't Av order Judah to join the celebration of Lev's return? How was his treatment of Judah similar to his treatment of Lev?

Going Inward

As a father, Av painfully allowed one son to do what he wanted. On the other hand, in unwavering affection, Av pleaded with his other son to enter into the joy of what was absolutely true—that Lev was still part of the family. In what way does Av's behavior help you understand what God is like? Set a timer for ten minutes and start writing about this question until the time is up. For your eyes only, don't worry about what comes out; just get your initial thoughts down.

Chapter 5 | What Happened Next . . .

Group Discussion

1. Did Av restore any of Lev's inheritance as part of receiving him back home? Why or why not?

2. What role do repentance, confession, and restitution play in our relationship with God and others? How are relationships affected if one or more of these is lacking?

3. Should repentance be required before a person is restored to a relationship, family, or church community? Should it be accepted as soon as an "I'm sorry" is offered, or tested over time to see if it's genuine?

Going Inward

You've read what we speculate could have happened after Jesus ended his story. Using your imagination, what do you think happened? Did Lev's experience permanently change him? Did Judah ever forgive Lev? Was the family rift ever healed? Why do you think you speculate in this direction? Set a timer for ten minutes and start writing about these questions until the time is up. For your eyes only, don't worry about what comes out; just get your initial thoughts down.

Afterword

Group Discussion

1. To what degree do you believe God's love extends to all people, regardless of what we believe or how we behave? In other words, is his love unconditional?

2. Given the verses that seem to point in opposite directions when it comes to the eternal destiny of humankind, on which outcome do you think the character of God and the weight of Scripture fall?

3. How does the idea of an eternal hell of conscious torment square with what the Bible teaches about God's love, grace, mercy, and justice?

Going Inward

We've listed twenty verses that at least imply God's love and forgiveness will be experienced by all humans, even though the "how to" is unclear. This is contradictory to the common Christian perception that God's justice requires satisfaction. Ask yourself: Where does this idea come from, and why? Set a timer for ten minutes and start writing about this question until the time is up. For your eyes only, don't worry about what comes out; just get your initial thoughts down.

THE BEHAVIOR SPECTRUM

If you would like to learn more about The Behavior Spectrum mentioned on page 43, scan the QR code below. It will take you to an animated presentation on the Christ in the Rockies website, where you can click through a series of slides.

ABOUT THE AUTHORS

Mike Haddorff (left) and Mike Hamel (right)

Mike Haddorff

I grew up in Fort Collins, Colorado, where I founded, operated, and eventually sold a generator business over a forty-year span. I've always had a teacher's mind. It's how I think. At an early age, I was able to develop and exercise this joy within the context of the church. I started teaching at Fort Collins Bible Chapel and today teach at our home church, Council Tree Covenant Church of Fort Collins.

In 2005, entirely out of left field and with the help of some very dear friends, we began Christ in the Rockies. CITR is designed to equip men to live an authentic

Christ-centered life. CITR pursues this mission by hosting camps for men of all ages in the Colorado Rockies. We also assist others in their efforts to provide outdoor adventure experiences for men of all ages.

I have always loved the outdoors. At this season, one of my interests is fly-fishing, specifically through instructing and guiding others in their journey within the sport. Sandra and I have been married since 1976. We have four grown children who still like to hang out with Mom and Dad.

Mike Hamel

Born in Kansas and raised in Denver, I served as a teaching pastor in churches in Colorado, Oregon, and Illinois. There, I also directed the Resource Center at Interest Ministries and briefly edited *Interest* magazine before hanging out my shingle as a freelance writer in 1996. Since then, I've written or substantially edited more than forty-five books on topics as wide-ranging as business, finance, political theory, health care, cancer, nonprofits, and religion. These include twenty books for children and young adults.

For the first half of my adult life, I was a preacher. For the second half, I've been a storyteller. I vastly prefer stories to sermons, especially children's stories. Preaching *tells* hearers what to think and how to act.

Storytelling *shows* readers how characters respond to certain situations and invites consideration.

My wife, Cindy, and I live in Colorado Springs, surrounded by a gaggle of grandkids. You can learn more about me at:

Christ ᴵᴺ ᴛʜᴇ Rockies

Seasoned Guides for the Masculine Journey

Christ in the Rockies (CITR) equips men of all ages to lead authentic Christ-centered lives. Our high-altitude camps and retreats offer the outdoor adventure of a lifetime, skillfully led by men with decades of life-guide experience.

High-adventure outdoor activities are designed for all skill levels and, depending on the camp, can include fly fishing, mountain biking, rock climbing, and rafting. Our in-depth teaching includes a blend of insights from Scripture, counsel from experts, testimonies from men with unique life experiences, as well as quiet time for personal reflection.

Mountaintop Experiences

We don't live on the mountaintop all the time, but mountaintop experiences can change how we live the rest of the time. Our camps and retreats

change lives. Just ask any of the hundreds of men aged 16 to 90 who have attended our events since 2007. We offer a wide range of camps and retreats specifically crafted for key times in the masculine journey:

- Passage to Manhood camps for fathers and sons
- Going Inward - Moving Onward camps for men 35 and older
- The Way of Wisdom camps for men 50 and older

Learn more about Christ in the Rockies, watch alumni testimonials, or sign up for one of our camps here.

Made in the USA
Las Vegas, NV
12 December 2023

82602425R10062